ELEMENTAL

Caitlin Press Inc.
8100 Alderwood Road,
Halfmoon Bay, BC V0N 1Y1
www.caitlin-press.com

Text and cover design by Vici Johnstone
Printed in Canada

Caitlin Press Inc. acknowledges financial support from the Government of Canada and the Canada Council for the Arts, and the Province of British Columbia through the British Columbia Arts Council and the Book Publisher's Tax Credit.

Library and Archives Canada Cataloguing in Publication

Braid, Kate, author
          Elemental / Kate Braid.
Poems.
ISBN 978-1-987915-63-1 (softcover)
          I. Title.

PS8553.R2585E44 2018 C811'.54 C2017-906530-0
PS8553.R2585E44 2018 C811'.54 C2017-906530-0

poetry

ELEMENTAL

Kate Braid

Caitlin Press

For all my family, each member of the clan —
rough and wide and raucous as that clan can be —
elemental to me

especially in memory of my mother, Mary Elizabeth,
and father, Harry Bernard — beloved.

"...everything was alive, not supernaturally, but naturally alive.... For the whole life-effort of [wo]man to get [her] his life into direct contact with the elemental life of the cosmos, mountain-life, cloud-life, thunder-life, air-life, earth-life, sun-life. To come into immediate *felt* contact and so derive energy, power, and a dark sort of joy."

— D.H. Lawrence

Contents

Water

AUTOBIOGRAPHY AS WATER

Saturday morning, Mother takes me to a chlorine-echoey box to learn
the lessons of deep water. I line up my small bathing-suited body at the
diving board and walk, heeding the siren call of shadows, white walls
that order, *Jump!* And am embraced into a world of green-glossed bubbles
and wonder. Until teacher snatches me back
to the sandpaper of breath and air.

SUDDEN SHOWER OVER SHIN-OHASHI BRIDGE AND ATAKE

By Hiroshige, 1857
Japanese woodblock print on paper

To be sewn to the earth by such a rain

  to be a part of the fabric,

    legs swinging wildly

       at a run,

    clothing

ripped by wind,

    this rain

a wilderness of pattern.

Nothing can cover me.

(Nothing can uncover me.)

Oh well. Oh well.

  Fisherman poles the boat another stroke

      closer   another stroke   closer

to our destination

    what we know

  is the bamboo

bridge beneath our feet

  this wind, the silk

    and stroke of rain.

VANCOUVER SPRING

Soggy under a glaze of wine,
the surreal grace of grass and moss
abundant
and another wet Vancouver sky.
It's spring, we say,
ubersweet, as we suffer
one more grey day.

When — if — the light finally shines,
we will rush out onto balconies
and bicycle paths,
spreading over sidewalks like puppies,
our eyes cast upward
to Sun.

Until then, it's another glass of wine
at the Sylvia Hotel, gazing out
at a grey beach, pedestrians with umbrellas,
black, walking, muttering,
It's spring!

LA SOURCE

By Jean Dominique Ingres, 1856
Oil on canvas

It's her feet that interest me, the pinky pallor of each small digit,
nails finely trimmed and reflected in the clear water
that tips from the urn on one white shoulder,
running over her hands, those feet.
But what woman has feet like that, smooth
as the alabaster of the marble columns one step away?

I look more closely. There's the necessary crease where her arm bends
but none at waist or hip or knee. Her lips are small and full, teeth
perfect porcelain peas in a small round mouth, the tiniest hint
of dark at her virgin mound. Nipples glow soft rose, breasts
a bare cup to the hand. Only the water that pours from her urn
spills like real water.

Any woman would laugh to paint such a picture.
Even the precise daisies and iris at her feet are virgin white.
But her toes, small peach pebbles — I like her toes.

LITTLE WIFE

She's been lying so long on the bottom of the sea
she's all caked over with chalcedony, shell
of oyster and clam. Her forehead is pearl, her ears
the curl of cockle shell. Fishes cast in green
swim through her long loose hair.

Beauty sleeps, encrusted. *Shhh!* people say, careful
not to wake her — so pure, so pretty,
no trouble, this little woman, little wife.

So what music, what rhythm of wave, of fin,
of storm above, what mariner's bell rings
almost too late, tremor that rocks her, calls her,
cracks her caul and whispers, *Time, at last, to wake!*

The Sunlit Sea Supports Nothing

The sunlit sea supports nothing but the shadows
cast by the outstretched wings of birds.
— Guillaume Apollinaire

They said I would be safe here.
Jesus (they said) walked on it.

But today when I ventured onto the sea
it was all flume and wind and

the high tops of waves until
I might have been reversed. Who knows?

It was blue all over, everything,
and a strange light threaded through

tying above to below. Did I mention the light?
It was a line threaded to my belly

and the sun — or was it the sea? — yanked it
from time to time, playing with me.

This water, it was saying,
this wind, this wave

take a deep breath. Trust us.

Tattoo

the proof of sea is fear.

— Alice Oswald

It takes longer than I thought to slip from one island to another,
slow gloss over water: blue slick, white slick. I skim
barely breaking through, splashes like scrawled code on my hands.
How long can I stand it, sunk in all this reflection?

Once I dove off the boat and almost couldn't get back.
Arbutus tossed messages of bark into the water,
instructions all around me but
I couldn't read them. Isn't there a language we share?

I trust only the hard white wheel under my hands,
a way to get somewhere. But I'm not making headway
try as I might, unanchored, my eyes shut tight,
blind from too much aluminum, too much light.

Water shines as if a porch light had been left on.
At home, under the dock, there are whispers (a far-away sound
through reeds.) Even the dead couldn't find me here
and everything has hooks. What once seemed so simple

is upside down. Buzz bomb, big-eyed jig; what's up?
What kind of highway has no yellow line to guide me
though buoys bob, trying to catch my attention
while the compass swings wildly. Isn't there a fixed point?

Should I turn back, or abandon all fear and
full speed ahead? Water carries me
a little further each day and I'm learning:
forward, reverse, come about.

That time I barely made it back into the boat?
When I finally stood, a small red tattoo of arbutus bark
clung to my left thigh. I've become a watcher now.
I'm studying codes.

UJI BRIDGE IN ISE

By Hiroshige, 1858
Japanese woodblock print on paper

What if a fisherman

what if
     his boat,

       a line

thin

    bamboo bridge beyond

and a mountain

     with high white tops

 regardless

     what if all the busyness

       of bridge

         and houses and trees, waiting

     a water taxi and

passing (in the distance

        a train

ever back   ever back

to here)

    this, what if

this fisherman

      a fish?

English as an Island

I stand on the edge of a braided black velvet sea,
sleek and dark as the hair of the woman
who swims here alone.

She will cross this ocean.
Someone brings food but she waves it aside saying
it's too bright, too full of light.

On this trip, she will drink the dark.
It's her voyage but
we're all strangely nervous.

We have come to see her off
but can't seem to find the right words —
everything is in a foreign tongue.

Already I can barely see her, her head
almost lost
over the raven-black shoulder of swells.

Stars sparkle like points of ice on dark water.
As if behind glass, the sea tips in tableau
as the wind begins to blow.

All we can do is wave and watch the black seas swell
and send our poor, thin English blessings after her,
like a weak light.

The Empty Cup

I wait
sitting in heat on the dusty ground

the bowl of my body open,
at attention.

A trembling cup
senses the approach of water.

All beings are grateful.
Somewhere far off, a bell rings

bird calls.

Somewhere far off, a bell rings.
All beings are grateful

for the approach of water,
the trembling cup.

At attention,
the bowl of my body opens.

Sitting in heat, on dusty ground
I wait.

Small Boat

*A gull racking the grey water
screams once, but no one answers.*

— E.G. Burrows

I.

I say I won't be afraid, swear
I'll get over this fierce fist to my gut
as the first roller rills under the boat
and I cast off my last tie
to land, leap aboard. I'm playing now —
this is my leisure. Say it again.

I swore I wouldn't be afraid, this time
I'd cast off, *fenders*
(I know the word, took the course),
curl the rope (*line*) carefully, stow it
where I can reach it again, quickly
and (I hope) soon, soon
as we reach the far shore. I swore

I wouldn't be afraid only you didn't tell me
there would be white caps and this upward diving
into a wilderness of water.
I watch you, all your senses poised
(I'm brilliant at the details)
knuckles on the boat's wheel, how you tense
into the next wave, bent forward not enjoying
the view, mountains fading.
Black breakers are my foreground now.

Conversation, when there is any,
is a polite fishing around. I stay away
from the terrors of the deep,
go shallow, then

it wasn't a sob just
small breath caught, I couldn't help it as I reached
for my rain jacket, something close and warm
and you noticed, said sharply,
You want to go back.

It wasn't a question.
I forgot courage, forgot promises, everything.
Yes, I said, *Yes,* and regretted it
too late, remembering it was a promise
too late but grateful anyway

as we headed back to a sliver of bright silver
hope, to the dock, the blessed shore. But I promise,
I promise, next time....

II.
And already the sea is lighter, sky clears.
There are no other boats — is this a sign?
Last night I dreamed my favourite gold earring dropped
in the water — is this another?

My heart, small pump, is overcome
by a dark sea of blood and unknown miles
of deep. Something is alive down there.
If I was thrown in the water, how soon
before deathly cold bit?

It doesn't matter how good a swimmer I am
there is nothing to save me
but a small curved bowl in the ocean,
a thin question mark of gasoline,
and a man's hand on the wheel
dissolving

MYSTERY

In memory of Heather Werner (1970 – 2005)

It is not a dark night. Moonlight spills like a web
over English Bay. Someone tells us
we have come to see spirits and though it's late,
it's bright as we tramp in single file
across a broken landscape (farm?
a ravaged field?) following the moon.
You are skeptical. I move as I'm told
to a small pillow of soil by the water.
What am I waiting for?
What does spirit look like?
Around me light has come and gone
and come again. There is a silky sheen to the air
when I notice a small object on the earth,
a bright copper penny. One. Then another, then
dozens, scattered like seeds. They are everywhere:
copper the colour of a woman's hair, copper
fallen in a mantle, pennies from heaven.
There is no mystery. This is how I know:
by the earth beneath my feet, by the heaving breast of sea,
by the small check mark of birds against the sky
I know this place, I can find it again. Everywhere now
I see it in the wave of poppies, blush of sunset,
red cheeks of apples. What was I worried about?
She is near, she is everywhere.

SWIMMING IN TIME

Is it because we all used to be
dolphins and whales
that now, slicing through water,
I feel my arms
gone to fins?

Mouthfuls of salt are easy on
my tongue, or is it
my nose? With the next long stroke
I forget about breathing
while my sides sizzle
with sapphire green bubbles.

No more envious of seagulls,
I search somewhere a sandy bank
for one good scratch
before I twist in a lazy curl
and dive for pearls.

LISTEN

It is night. Outside
a light across the blind
and the wet rubber sound
of a car passing.
Bamboo sings a long song
to the wind
and the house sighs.
Rain drops like a shawl.

Fire

Autobiography As Fire

A clumsy child, I burned myself
a hundred times.
Summer camp brought the promise of skill.
Find stone, the Girl Guide leader said.
Find wood.
Now the epic of the wet and the dry,
careful crossing of sticks, rubble
of a tiny cabin,
twig upon twig
(oh balance, come to me now).
Precious furniture of birch bark and a small mountain
of matches
until finally a flame,
and I grow warm inside a larger circle.

MONOLITH

I.

They must have been moving her —
five feet of polished grey stone
with a wild auburn streak where the crack is.
Now she lies broken, the ropes still upon her
with two men untying, bulldozer panting behind.

She might have been the perfect monolith
for water to run over or flowers to cascade down.
Instead she lies dug up, just another inconvenience
to those who live on the surface.
Like a crow mourning, I circle. And again
for another look. Notice how she still burns.

II.

I read once that natives of the Amazon mountains
choose shamans at birth, raise them inside a mountain
preparing them. Children who have never seen day
are only told the power of light until the morning
of their nineteenth birthday when they're led

in ancient ritual to the door of the highest cave

and taken outside to watch their first sun rise.

III.

Can you imagine how it feels
to be hauled from darkness
and no matter how much it aches,
to be swathed in light?

LIKE THE ROCK

Like the rock
      we are broken
like the fire
      fiercely burn

occasionally
      we may even shine
as reflections
      caught, for a moment

small lights
      that gleam here and now
we may even flow
      as song.

A Photograph of Her When She Was Three

After Adrienne Rich's "Diving Into the Wreck"

Her eyes are dark and wide and serious.
She is in a new house in a new city.
She has a new brother
and the world feels precarious,
one-legged. The dark around her.

A flashbulb pops, startling her
as she looks into the brightness.
Standing, playing debonair
on one chubby leg, leaning
against that old coffee table (remember?)
in front of a fireplace that holds no fire.

There is no anchor where she stands
on that small leg.
At four she will develop a strange ailment
of the same leg, spend months unable to walk,
carried everywhere. But that is later.
Now, she leans against glass
staring wide-eyed into the camera
looking.

The eye behind the camera does not ask her to smile,
or has she already refused? Behind her dark eyes
there are more important things she must consider —
like the balance of the world, its emptiness,
its lack of fire.

LAVA

*If the mountain spewed stones of fire into the river
it was not taking sides.*

— Adrienne Rich

Think of me as your heart's blood

one day slow, unheeded, inevitable
as an underground river

next day bursting margins, veins,
boundaries.

Think of me as your future
flowing, not etched —

not yet

all
yearning toward a dark potential.

Move closer. Don't be afraid.
We are all rock, all stone.

All you can do now
is ride this current

and remember
we are all transforming

more or less slowly,
more or less within the lines.

SILENCE

All day you have craved silence,

the quiet not just of no other body,
not even one going about its business *sans* talk

nor even another body sleeping. No.
You snap at your beloved and when he finally leaves

on some errand, you know
you have craved exactly this,

to be alone, in this space,
with only largeness around you.

So now it is here and what's wrong?
Silence sits, not alive, not awake and waiting

not open, no.
Leaden, it sits.

This silence doesn't want soft music
or the luxury of a silly computer game.

It doesn't even want chocolate.
What then?

Slowly it dawns — this silence wants
the uncertainty of a candle. You light one, two,

take a deep breath under the movement of shadow,
flicker of flame licking a simple cotton wick,

going nowhere
except here

as you sink into the chesterfield, a book,
the fierce flicker of your thoughts, companioned.

Opening the Cabin

I.

We have come to the cabin after weeks
in the smoke of city living, climb out of the car,
crisp with caution. Peering suspiciously up at sunshine
we sniff the honey of cedar and pine.

Small trickles of ease as we open windows, sweep.
It is in moving that our bodies come to know
where we are.
The neighbour waves and our faces light.

II.

We lie on the bed, reading. You, British history and I,
the collected poems of Jane Kenyon.
Fire crackles and pings in the stove
while rain chimes over our heads.
It's noon and we've been lying like this,
reading the odd passage to each other, content,
lost in our books most of the morning.

Now your breathing deepens, the book slips and you sleep.
Across the room, green cedar sways lightly
through the big windows. Rain freshens. A blue jay squawks.
You snore a little. The poet might say,
I was overcome with a fierceness of joy.
I touch your side, feeling only wonder.
The fire snaps and sings.

Wood

AUTOBIOGRAPHY AS WOOD

On the raw edge of town I discovered them, hid for hours
in their leafy dark. Their unbuiltness, open to anything, made me want
to build — a wall, a roof — then take it down. Over and over the labour of
saplings, endlessly leaning them against each other in clean air, joined.
I made space for a door, a window. From inside, looked out.

Younger Sister

She hung around her father, this one, liked
the low dusky shed where he planed lazy curls
off sweet-smelling cedar.

A curious child, no one sent her to school
but somehow she learned
in the glow of late afternoons
when her father, resting, would answer
her endless questions. Watching him,
she rocked back and forth singing,
learned by mime
the rhythms of his trade.

Her mother caught her there often
running her fingers over the fine ribs, reading
the message left by the wood plane's passage.
Chased back to the kitchen over and over
the girl returned 'til finally
she was left in peace with her father.

He had given up teaching his son.
The boy couldn't settle down,
wanted to be out all day, talking in the Temple
instead of learning his trade. The father accepted
his daughter instead, showed her
how the tools worked for her,
let her hold the end of the fine woods
he carved into shelves and furniture,
the odd cross.

When first the girl picked up a chisel
and touched it to wood, it responded
like flesh to her fingers.

More patient than her brother
who figured he had to do everything
before he was thirty, she carved flowers and animals,
let dumb wood speak. Neighbours came,
stood around in crowds to watch, said,

34

The child performs miracles
with wood. You would swear
she brought dead animals to life,
made wooden flowers bloom.

Now sometimes you see her alone in her shop
in a bath of cedar-scented air
sharpening the edges of her tools
or resting, studying her folded hands
callused and cut,
the scars on her palms.

For Jude, the Cabinetmaker, in His Shop

Is it so strange to think of this as sacred space,
here, as we talk of whether cut trees are alive or dead,

how their cells, like ours, need water.
But after death, I mean

after being cut, or fallen,
when they swell and twist and shrink —

is it life? Who else can I ask
such an important, such a pressing question?

Which brings us to how trees give off a gas or is it a hormone
that soothes humans as we walk among them, how

people, given difficult mental puzzles, do better after they have walked
in forest. How needy we are and don't know it.

The forester says
if disease strikes a tree at one side of a forest, the rest

simultaneously make antibodies. Like a cathedral,
one pillar relying on every other to create a sacred space

each element in touch, alive — moulds to roots to leaves to creatures
visible and invisible, trees and mosses, insects and birds.

Is this what we call holy, this connection of the whole,
each to every other?

Which brings us to the silence of the island where we live —
hush of wind, cry of birds, whistle and run of trees

as loud as any city street when you listen.
If you listen.

Which bring us to the two slabs of maple
in front of us as we stand — the lumber dusty, its cells long dried

since they fell and came to stand here, in your carpenter's shed.
Do they know they've been chosen

for some small human's pleasure, to grace a wall as sculpture, as art?
Is that why I run my hand over them again and again, saying hello?

Or is it asking permission perhaps, as we discuss
which side, which length, how thick.

We keep our distance, say "board," say "lumber," say "wane"
staying far from the breath, the memory of branch and leaf,

say "inches" and "feet," hardly noticing
the workshop is suddenly hushed, as if alert

as if all the other trees — posts and beams — are listening
as this one prepares to leave.

—◊—

When asked if they'd ever felt "watched" in a forest,
a roomful of people raises their hands.

And was it animals watching? the questioner asks.
Oh no, every soul responds. Not animals, but trees.

Twenty-five years since I too, worked with wood.
Now, breathing sawdust in your shop,

I see how I have missed exactly this — these trees, their company.
My fingers itch for another rough handshake, *Hello, Hello*!

It's been too long without old friends.

The Wood Hanging

For Jude Farmer

It was an innocent wish — to have
a piece of wood around her bathtub,
something with the original waney edge
("live edge" the carpenter would call it)
something to remind her of forest close up.
So it was done and that night she took a bath
with the wood — an old, old maple — hanging beside her.

It wasn't then, in the bustle and focus of soap and water.
It was later — she'll blush in the telling.
It was late in the night when she stumbled
half asleep into the bathroom

and felt a presence, glanced over at the tub —
where lay a tree, a huge being alive
with wane and grain and history,
a Moby Dick of fallen disaster and majesty,
an up-and-down of history, a living Ark
floating over her wall and on, it seemed, up
into a stream of legend and story originating in a swamp
("somewhere nearby" the carpenter had said).

"It looks like the Hudson Bay," he'd said that afternoon
as they stood, fixed, watching it settle against her wall.
He was pointing to a fissure in the wood's edge.
"And here's the Canadian Shield," she'd said,
running her fingers over a tightness of grain nearby.

The next day she will tell him, "That wood has character."

Yes. A novel's worth, a whole library.
"There will be many stories," the carpenter had said.
And tonight, now, in the half-dark of a nightlight,
the tree — with the slightest creak of an accent — has begun.
There will be many stories.
She looks forward to hearing them, all of them.
It will take a lifetime.

Fairy Tale

> In this fairy tale,
> we go to the woods together,
> admire the trees in velvet dresses
> woman trees, their sex obvious.
>
> —Linda Rogers, "Hot Air"

Like very good girls
we imagine this as mere play,
put on our best dresses, frills and pink
for the visit. The Mrs.
Cedar and Pine are "in" today.
Our tea shall entail
pine nut paté, dew in tiny brown cups.
We leave home entranced, hail
to this fairy tale.

No one told us it might rain,
that we wouldn't get home for supper,
that we should have brought supplies:
flashlight, rations, a pencil
in case we needed to write home to mother.
We weren't prepared for rough weather.
You scold me. As the eldest sister
it's always my fault. Bickering
passes the time as we walk the path, lined in heather. At least
we go to the woods together.

Once we teach each other to see through thick brush
we're surprised at what we find.
Of course, there are the ordinary flowers
that politely point us on our way
and hardly any (except the morning glory,
jealous of our independent path), cause us stress.
Mostly we find green moss and green ground glowing
with salal, grape ivy and roots.
We pause to take a picture of vines thick as tresses,
admire the trees in velvet dresses.

This is a grown-up place
where vines caress the branches they languish on.
Just watching them, our breasts grow warm.
We forget to hold hands
as a tree crashes down, pine
embracing the earth in front of our eyes, her surrender copious.
In the sudden light of it, we can see
the silk of tree bark, branch touching branch,
an ecstatic, shivering forest of evergreens, delirious
woman trees, their sex obvious.

MASTERS OF THE EARTH

Do you know? Don't you wonder?
What's going on down under you?

— David Crosby

Masters of the earth, when you shelter
under a tree in a storm,
place your ear against its bark:

listen as it sings
in a long wild key while roots, like toes,
scramble under you.

Seismologists can't test during storms
because the movement of tree roots
distorts sound.

So while wind whips rain 'round your head
and you take these trees for givens,
remember you lean your ear against a living friend
and be careful.

THE DIMENSIONS OF LUMBER

A two-by-four is a cut and damaged tree.
How much does it remember?

When it is captured under a Duroid roof
does it miss sky?

Or if the roof is cedar, does it feel
less alone?

When closed inside the tight and airless closet
of a plastic and plaster wall, sealed off

according to the Building Code
from the entry of bird or sunshine or wind

then in that glooming dark
does it imagine it is home again in a smaller trunk?

Or does it feel confined as a nun, wild one
turned wall-dweller, anchoress of the domestic?

Does it call?
And is it calling now, here, silently,

inside the heedless purgatory
of these, my own four walls?

CARPENTER: TO THE TREES

> You can't help but think a table is a good use of a tree.
> To build it, a carpenter need not feel ashamed of pounding
> nails into wood.
>
> — Lorna Crozier

Have I hurt you? Or perhaps,
how have I hurt you? Or

is it an exchange we make:
               I will build myself a house,
                  a table, a bed,
and one day my ashes will nourish
your seed

and so the bargain will be fulfilled?

This week I ate meat and vegetables
with pleasure and one day
my ashes shall nourish these too.

But have I hurt you?

Such beauty under my hands. I have loved
grain and knot, given thanks for shelter.
If you continue to bend
under my touch, is it enough that
I continue to love you?

Is it enough?

I gather small hearts —
twig of arbutus, knot of fir —
to place on my table.
My shelves and window sills
are patterned with them.

I read once that anything we pay attention to
becomes sacred.

But is it enough?

TREE SONG

> *Naked trees extend their complicated praise*
> *branches sway, in*
> *a sort of unison*
> *not agreed upon*
> *each their own way*

> — John Terpstra, "Naked Trees"

May I be forgiven, may I forgive
myself this endless search for someone, some
thing to explain, give me the reason we're here
and what lies after and if there's a plan
(or even better) Planner — if I could only
know for sure (just once? a deal? I'll stay
right here, you whisper in my ear, The Answer...)
while all around me animals carry on
regardless. Plants and insects don't bother counting days
and naked trees extend their complicated praise.

Why them? How can they praise and not await
reward? Who do they praise? What? How
can they stand there, splendid, and not ask why or if
there is a goal? at least a prize
for the very best? Do they dream of after-death or fear
old age or insects or men with saws? Can it matter
that underneath the soil they're all in touch —
what one knows, all know instantly in a deciduous,
coniferous vocabulary that whispers a grace, as all around
branches sway in a sort of unison.

Perhaps I should sit and watch, listen
for a while, to the shushing of trees,
peace in one place, a salute to sky
and no complaints unless you count the crack
of the final fall and what do they see then?
Is there mortal terror? Or a welcome to the stones
they shall now lie upon, the bed from which to nourish
other trees? If we die childless are we
forgotten? Is heaven a tonic
not agreed upon?

Some say there's nothing to be frightened of,
there's God or gods or goddesses or not, to take me "home"
or not. I'll find out soon enough, that's sure.
Perhaps this is my fascination with birds
who fly above, rest lightly on each moment,
small prayers to the beginning and end of day.
And after all, how can it matter that I get the story right
or wrong? When it comes to living — life and death —
each being sings a sort of roundelay,
each their own way.

GREY

By Emily Carr, 1931– 32
Oil on canvas

Lawren warned this wouldn't be easy,
ripping open a great cedar's heart
with only my own

pinpoint precision.

Cedar's heart is nothing soft after all,
no round shoulder to cry on, no.

Cedar's heart is pure triangle, sharp
corners shockingly mathematical,
three sides wrapped round each other
and a glimpse of space, endless
inside all those arms
equilateral, algebraical.

After that it's nightmares, waving:
Come. Closer. If you dare.

Promises.

I dream I am stripped to the core.
There's a cold wind, grey eye
that sees everything.

Only that.

LULLABY FOR A SICK FATHER

Papa, as I stand over your bed I close my eyes
and dream back to construction days, feel
the grain of my fingers, their memory
of pitch and sawdust, and wish
that trees could move for you

and it is so.

In darkest night, a British oak, sweet cedar,
a powerful Douglas fir and the graceful arbutus
shift, stand quietly now
at the four corners of your hospital bed.

You are already small
as they extend their roots, their branches
gently, meet and form a net, a living web
beneath you. No one notices
as your hospital bed lifts
one leg then another until
as though in a hammock
you sway, a child again, rocking.

You are not alone.
Four guardians, posted at the corners
of your heart-heightened world
lift, their humming lives transferred
like a current, their pulse now pounding for yours.

Do you feel it, a transfusion of nectar and green?
You settle and sigh into a swaying peace,
given breath drawn deep from the earth, from sky.

Birds come.
There is a small cutting and travel of beetles,
whisper of bud and flower and leaf,
a breeze of fervent green.

You dream
deep handholds of bark, your strength
the smooth arms of arbutus and you rest
in greatness. No matter what happens now
you are safe.

BEING TREE

For Christine Lowther

I remember being tree, rising.
I remember the community of roots,
branches, green-twinned
to creatures.

The relief of it.

I remember a single pulse
in the wild shows of fall —
oh you maples! you oak! —
tickle of birds, mice, bats,
rampaging humans.

Power of sap rising.

And when we fall?
The suck of new growth, life rising over.

Inside Mother Roof

> All terms found in the Glossary of *Japanese Joinery: A Handbook for Joiners and Carpenters.*

I.
The way of the tree,
key connection, key.

Cuts heart
wing wood entangled.

One thousand bird wings approach.
Praying hands making wood

weave a many-roofed room
harmonizing chipped parts.

Small dance
inside mother roof.

Inside mother roof
small dance

harmonizing chipped parts
weaves a many-roofed room.

Praying hands.
One thousand bird wings approach

wing wood entangled.
Cut heart.

Key connection, key,
the way of the tree.

II.
Wild rafter about to drop!
Hip of a man's kimono pants sweep out window.
Too much trouble board.

III.
Approach three-and-a-half roofs
back properly straight.

Looking at centre
weave room,
bridging heaven place.

Small dance.
Enter centre, worship female wood.

Sky

AUTOBIOGRAPHY AS SKY

I took a single breath, reluctant; sharp red and silver scratching
at new-born cells, first fierce welcome to a new world.
Years later I lifted into air, flew for hours between a rising moon
and a setting sun — furious silver, furious red. As the two fought
over the lighting of the stage and clouds changed the scenery
over and over, I understood the drama of sky. At last.

CROW: 1

A hard hollow thump on my front step
brings me from breakfast
to the porch where a crow hops,
oddly unafraid, too close
to the screen door and the human behind it, her hand
on the latch.

Red drops scatter over the porch floor
like food colouring but thicker,
crow's blood pumping from his left foot.
What has he come for — sympathy? help?
a dry place under the eaves to rest?

He cocks his head, looks at me. What is the question?
The answer? He won't say, or I am too startled to listen.
He thumps another tattoo on the screen
and I am afraid to open it.
When he turns and flies away, only then
I open the door, call out.

THE BIRDS

All the birds are waiting:
eagle on an abandoned post in the river
that once anchored barges of logs,
heron that startles as it flies fast, low
at the level of my eyes as I drive off the ferry.
All of them are impatient for something
they saw long ago, something
we humans with our pitifully poor eyes, weak hearts,
something we can't seem to see.

Can't. Don't. Won't.

The chickadees and house sparrows twitter about it —
you might almost say angry — at the feeder.
The red-headed woodpecker knocks himself silly
trying to wake us up. Owls, gulls, crows —
no matter how hard they screech its name
we are impervious, deaf, dumb and blind
like weather vanes, so lost
in the bright moment's breeze
that we hardly notice
the dark direction in which they point.

REDWING, I SAY

> *Sparrow, we say, redwing, magpie, crow.*
> *The field goes on.*
> — Maureen Scott Harris

Redwing, blackbird, able feeder,
what do you have to teach me?

Forgive my demand. It is based on urgency.
I do not say *desperate* but you will understand.

Redwing, bearing your own epaulettes,
unspeakable courage to always fly

forward. Are you not tempted sometimes to return
to the egg?

Redwing, why did the one who named you
omit the gold, the sun that shines from you to light the way?

Or is it your song that leads, gives me courage,
tricks me, some days, into looking up. Just this.

FIELDS OF SKY

The hammerhead crane is the stork of the trades.
Feet forever anchored to a concrete shore, head
swinging back and forth, back and forth
in city-pitted air, it calls
a mechanical, yearning honk
to each passing bird.

The hammerhead crane gives warning
there's more, more to come. Next year
when this space is filled with thirty-two stories
of concrete and steel, what will a bird do then,
flying in smaller and smaller circles, looking for its own kind
in these ever-narrowing fields of sky?

SUPERMAN

With thanks to the Cowboy Junkies

It's getting harder to hide his identity. Close calls.
He wants to touch down, stop hiding
behind the glass of phone booth walls. It isn't fun anymore.
He was trying to go higher (escape) and all along
the power lay right beneath his feet.
Dear dirt. Who knew?

Superman has trouble with boundaries.
All that air space and no doors to close behind him, no traffic lights,
no yellow line to divide the going from the coming. Even the sea
has a shore. What does he really want? Did anyone ask?
Did Jimmy? Cub reporter soooo excited to be seen with a Real Hero?
Or Lois? Called herself his girlfriend, yearning for the Hunk,
the Prize, the perfectly Unattainable.

If anyone had asked, he would have told you
how tired he was. All that rescue.
Imagine him sprawled in a deckchair at last, doing nothing,
beer in hand, barbeque.
Give the guy a break or he'll break. He's getting older now,
creases at his knees, the odd hole in his uniform,
corners of those bright eyes, fading.

Superman wants to come in from the cold, home
to a fireplace where he can hang up that silly outfit,
trade it for beige bathrobe and slippers, slide
into the brown leather armchair he always yearned for.
A nice cup of tea, two candles on the mantle
and no wind in his ears, just the crackle of fir in the fire
and somewhere a clock ticking, gentle rain
as he sleeps — dry — his feet come to rest on earth
at last.

Airplane Whine

It used to be simple. You sat while someone brought you hot dinner on a tray, silver cutlery, linen. *More coffee?* You rested, reading, often watching out the window an unravelling blue.

Now it's one cramped seat in front of the other, jostling knees and full combat over who gets to jam all three pieces of their matching luggage plus the precious (monster) vase for Aunt Maud that CAN NOT BE CRUSHED into the tiny overhead bin, first. You pack your carry-on around your feet. Think plaster cast.

Now it's no food, *So sorry!* except water and a stale pretzel but to divert you, your own private screen. *It's Free!* but *Not working today, so sorry.* Audio then? You get Bon Jovi though you were thinking Elvis. You glance outside — a burst of blue as you change the music to "Going Deep" by Eli Bay. It's called Meditainment and promises perfection before Toronto.

Are we there yet?

But here's the classical section and it's OK, there's Water Service, for free if you ring the red button. So you plug in, tap Bach, only one ear phone doesn't work but you've accidentally hit Alternative Rock, all hands off now except the one that must hold (back to Bach) the ear plug to your oddly too-large ear but now the Captain announces 30,000 birds going by (did he say that?) and you're lost, your feet in a block of plaster, one finger in your ear and up to your eyeballs in choice, dreaming of the old days until finally you settle on Joni Mitchell, classic enough for now, turned on like a radio, when a casual glance over your shoulder —

and there, a silver line of azure meets Scheherazade. There's a world outside your window, an exotic roll of sapphire and silver, a cobalt and pearl panorama where fancy can wander unleashed, no earplugs, no button necessary. You sit back, stunned at the beauty of it, a marvel that was there all along while you were inside too busy reading small screens, too close to find satisfaction in spite of the pretzels, the water they gave you, for free.

CROW: II

I.
The relief of green
and one small, black

dot
of crow

teaching me
the words

karaoke
of landscape.

II.
Along the way, crow becomes
a shadow companion;

colleague, escort
reminder

guardian crow.

III.
There are things you cannot
explain —

how crows fly over rock
soil, sorrow

anything you're hauling.

IV.
The round chorus of their
calls, *Cras! Cras!*

the Romans heard as
Tomorrow! Tomorrow

v.
It all goes in a circle:
the coming and going

simple

as a mountain is simple
as sea.

SHE SITS,

a drizzle day.
This is what it's like
to be buried

in grey,
shrouded
in lead.

Even rock
shines
under rain.

Above her
there's a rustle
in black cedar

and a robin
(red)
sings.

First there's the flood in the new apartment. "Lucky you hadn't finished moving in," the insurance adjuster says cheerfully. "Makes it easier to move you out while we fix the floors." Then it's a second leak, found the same morning as the floor layers arrive — and of course, promptly leave — calling back, "Let us know when you find the leak!" Then the only elevator breaks ("Nothing moves till it's fixed!") and there's nothing she can do but walk out into rain, to end up in the park staring at the flat black of a pond where movement catches her eye and up from nowhere, a flash of small birds that flutter, rise and fall together like a silk scarf shaken clean. She watches as they reach the far side of the water, rise over cedars and disappear. The air feels lighter when they are gone.

BREATH

The world lies very still. Inside, the high hum of the wood fire burning. My lover turns to get comfortable as he reads on the double bed. Outside, trees stand hushed. They have let out all their green until the world is one colour under cloud; no wind, not a leaf stirs, no insect.

The neighbour hasn't noticed. Every few minutes there's a tap of his hammer but slowly, as if he struggles against some inertia, can't say why his hammer is suddenly so heavy. A robin lights on thick moss, fire outside my window. He poses for a moment and then as if a signal, ignited, sun breaks through, boughs wave, hammer gets busy.

The world only needed the weight of a bird for it all to begin again. Inside, breakfast dishes sit unwashed on the kitchen counter. My hand at the table opens around a cooling cup of coffee.

Calgary Stampede: 1956

Hint of horse dung in the wide Prairie air, ghost of tepees as one by one
we children follow our father, stranger we rarely see, into the silence of the
Hudson's Bay Company Linen Department past dark heaps of tablecloths,
bath towels, sheets, through a narrow door marked "Staff Only!" hearts
pounding beneath our newly pressed genuine cowboy shirts, fringed fake
leather jackets, the shadow of my brother's Stetson spread like a shawl
across little boy shoulders.

We enter the place our father calls Work, expanse of dark desk half-lost
under a sludge of paper, a wooden chair or two, walls of grey files waiting
while he clears a path so he can lift us one by one to the window ledge —
the usual warnings — and open it wide.

There's a quick handshake to three stories of clear air, luminous in the July
morning before we lean far over, disobeying every rule to press small hands
onto cool stone and sway, glorious above red and yellow clowns who scoop
up the horse dung. We wave at silver majorettes and marching bands and
the mayor, waving back, and best of all, the *clop clop* of hooves and the
majesty of Cree and Shawnee and Sarcee, grand on their mounts, rich and
mysterious with beads and real leather, the sharp tang of horses like lemon.

It happens every year like a wish, that on this one jewel of a day, Father gifts
us with the magic of height, leads us aloft like birds to hover alone with him
in blue sky, breathless.

Earth

AUTOBIOGRAPHY AS EARTH

Constant before, no matter how I stepped on it, I loved the deep rift
in the earth of our street, explored it while everyone else went in,
obedient, to supper. Later the neighbours would say I fell, but no,
I entered it. This is what it feels like to be stone in the landscape of dark,
to be buried and rise again. When Mother pulled me out, I looked back,
saw the flicker of heat below, earth calling quietly, *Come.*

The Day of the Carr Family Farm Auction

Southern Alberta, 1993

Remember that day, the people from the community
coming just to be there because, as the minister says,
The more of us there are, the higher the prices go,
and Betty reminding you they're selling voluntarily
because otherwise one of them will die from stress;
far better than the bank auctions where no one bids high
and the seller is twice humiliated.

Remember the plain scaredness Doug admitted later,
that today, twenty years of their work would be judged. Today
they might lose everything
as Betty stops to welcome the man who
for all those years sold them fertilizer and chemicals,
now come all the way from Edmonton to say thank you,
goodbye.

Remember the Hutterite, dark raven with his black cap
pulled low against the cold, clear spotlight of space around him
as he hovered over the freshly painted augur.
Remember him hitching it to his truck to take home,
the shadow of a smile as he drove past

and the man who sat all day in the green John Deere,
who'd exclaimed to Doug just the night before,
Why would an old guy like me want a giant like this!
in love with a big green tractor
that after fifteen minutes of hair-raising bidding
he wins, and grins.

Remember the young man who told Betty with tears in his eyes
how he'd looked forward to May like Christmas
so he could drop by the Carr farm for more seed,
more laughter.
Remember all the old farmers with tears in their eyes
remembering their own auctions.

The relief.

Remember the 640 hot dogs sold by the Women's Institute
and so much coffee, they lost track of which was the decaf,
all the tables sinking under homemade pies, apple and rhubarb,
sweet and sour for an auction,
and the hired man who kept talking about a new start for himself
with tears in his eyes
and young Bill coming home to see the house he was born in,
empty now, and asking to sleep there, one last night,
on the bare kitchen floor with Emmy, the dog
while Sara, sixteen, helped to pack
every last piece of their life into brown boxes.

The sisters and brothers who have come by plane
to say *Hello, Goodbye,* burst into tears all together,
then laugh at their crying.

Remember Betty worrying about Doug,
Doug worrying about everything else,
and the few women bidding while their husbands work
full time in town for the cash to keep their own farms going
a little longer, and the farmer in the Bluejays baseball cap
who watches the sky, barley running through his fingers
as if absent minded, as if all his senses weren't concentrated now
as he smells it, chews it, tastes quality under a brilliant sunshine,
harsh clean cold that keeps spirits up and the ground hard so
more trucks can come and farmers buy,
and the tears in Doug's eyes when Betty tells him
about all the others with tears in their eyes, strong faces lined
by weather and squinting, as if into dust, trying to say *love*
on the land when it's not easy.

Remember the auctioneer saying this is the best auction
he ever held because the equipment is so cared for
and old Einer coming in on Betty and Sara and the minister,
all crying and laughing together and Einer nodding approval,
That's what you gotta' do.

Remember the prayers, even if you don't pray that way,
and Norman, the father, a week before he dies, stroking
Doug's hand saying, *I'm proud of you, son,* with his eyes
and Doug excited about his new job as consultant

and Betty already studying to go back to nursing,
what she always wanted, she says, if she couldn't farm.

Remember them now, prayers as ritual, framing an end
and a beginning and Marie, the mother, jumping to her feet,
asking the minister to bless this family, please
while everyone stands, holds hands and prays
Amen, meaning, "to strengthen,"
Amen, meaning, "may it be so."
Remember *Amen.*

BLACKBERRIES FOR JACQUELINE

After your wake, I go outside to walk. It's the perfect time for blackberries, late August after a hot summer. The island roads are lined with bushes hung with dark stars ready to explode and soon I am buried in a blackberry bush, my hands the colour of wine.

It reminds me of the time we worked together, building the house from which I have just wished you farewell. Usually the clients cooked, but on the night we finished the roof, you and I dressed in our best blue jeans and went to the poshest restaurant in town, ordered a whole bottle of red wine; to hell with good sense and early risings!

We drank to each other's health, to the house we were building, to wine glittering in crystal goblets lit by an island sunset. And as the wine took hold we joked about twin tattoos, what we would want, and where. We loved each other that night for being so silly and so strong. We always planned to do that again.

Now the fierceness of thorns has torn my favourite jeans. It's the berries, hanging just beyond my reach. I reach further.

That was the job where someone left a spike in the concrete and when we stripped the walls it caught me square on the bare shoulder as I hurried along, conscious only of the planned, not the unplanned. When you saw the blood you said, *The tattoo has chosen you. Now you'll never forget this job.* It was the last time we worked together.

Now I choose the most perfect berry, fat and black and so sweet, I taste perfume. I hold it to the sun, a toast, then fling it into the light for you, Jacqueline, wherever you are.

On the last night of that job, the cook promised our favourite — blackberry and peach pie — if we picked the berries. We'd dashed out laughing, daring each other to fill the pail. You scolded me then, for eating every second one, for being unable to resist.

The next berry, I eat. The next, I throw to you. We are picking together, you and I, as we did all those years ago. My hands and mouth are wet, my eyes. Dark juice runs up my wrists to my elbows. My clothes are stained purple.

Drink, my friend. Tonight we celebrate again, just as we promised. Tonight, a toast to all the great and good women we have known, women we have loved.

Wood Buffalo National Park

For Mary Ann Bibby

This is the world impenetrable, the flat
black pupil that doesn't look at you

Sue Sinclair, "Big East Lake"

…only it does
look.
You've come here because
friends insist you see a buffalo
and you're too polite to say no.

You've seen dozens on TV, you argue —
all those Westerns — but you go anyway,
and when a herd appears on a nearby crest,
shift impatiently in your seat. Done. Let's go.
No, no, they urge. *Get closer.*

So you approach the mesh fence.
The others return to the car, sated
but something has caught you, the thick brown butter
of one buffalo, separate from the herd,
who stays as the others rumble off.

You bend, hunched near the fence, your eye brighter
as he steps, one foot, two, closer
to where you crouch, having made yourself into some
not-so-human shape, you hope,
smaller   breathless   waiting

for the beauty of him, his massive shoulder.
You are struck dumb with love, with wonder at his tiny back,
as if vision had suddenly faltered and is microscoped
under the mountainburst of those shoulders, that head.

Closer

he comes. You hardly breathe, hardly dare wonder why
he bothers. You carry no food.
Is it because he has something to say, perhaps?

71

Because he wants to see you too?
A dream you've shared?

Three steps away, he stops.
You can't smell him, only
fix on the side of his massive head
where one luminous black eye holds you,
a lake, alive with everything
you ever wanted to know   here.

Maybe if you wait he will bless you.

But no. He moves off, too soon, too
graceful for such a huge creature and you
are left, abject, awkward, stick-thin
and still not knowing

but closer.

MOSS AND STONE

Where you stumble, there lies your treasure.

— Joseph Campbell

How can it be other than innocent, this ancient down-leading ramp
    once carved, now cushioned in a foam of moss undisturbed by time?

I am stone-launched into earth.
    Alone I descend, daring my friends, *Who knows what we'll find?*

But they only wave, anxious, lost behind green moss
    as I push through a wood and heavy door hinged in a rusty tongue

into a stone-grey room. There's a glimpse of granite before I stumble hard,
    a dark lens of terror sucking me into the heart of rock.

Flailing, desperate, I remember now; I was here before. I fell then, too.
    Everyone who enters must fall, obedient to earth.

Memory vanishes, mere names. Somewhere above me, a clear light holds.
    When I raise my head, I see The People gathered on grey stone benches

in a circle of silence. I have come to the place of critical counsel.
    There is the smell of dry earth packed and no sound, no sound at all.

One woman, dressed in something loose and grey,
    takes my trembling hand to raise me to my feet.

The sureness of her step, firm grip, lift me and I see now
    blocks of granite, edges softened by time.

My coat hangs open, the buttons — connection — gone. I shake, as with cold,
    and the woman, seeing the damage, with her strong fingers mends it.

Here is no logic that I know, nor speech, only The People, magisterial
    in a circle and a connection that hums sub-lingual, all senses combined

in a conversation of colour and shape that is the swarm of insects, creep of lichen,
    language in russet and diamond, fall of water, emerald of the leaping heart;

here are the eloquent lines of mathematical equation, mosaic of silence and bodies
    vibrating, whole, each in tune with every other.

The woman leads me to the centre of the circle where I stand, trembling
before a small wooden chest of sweet and frozen memories.

The man who guards it invites me to witness, touch its guiding device.
Remember the cold of that time, he asks, *when people put their seeing*

in the deep freeze? Out of the chest he lifts, reverently, instruments
wrapped and silent now. *Gifts of the past,* he says.

Air is silver with the hum of a power remote, unquestionable, but a young woman
interrupts, raucous, reaches a hand out and takes.

Her careless grab and sandpaper laugh see only entertainment, seize it on a whim.
She points the instrument, presses it, heedless in suddenly clamorous air.

The People wait, hidden, eternally patient. When I wake, trembling, there is a taste
of new moss and earth in my mouth and a voice saying, *This is a time to mourn.*

To the Coal Miner Buried Alive

I am the untamed earth who bites,
leaves scars on darkness.

I am rock's slow
hot breath.

Feel the inhale   exhale
on your cheek

light shining blue
all around you.

I will embrace you,
take you with me

to terror and darkness.
My voice rumbles

promising
we will lean against fire.

SEAMS OF SOUND

For Don Mowatt, retired CBC radio producer *extraordinaire*;
for the Men of the Deeps, the Cape Breton, Nova Scotia, men's
coal-mining choir; and for their director, Jack O'Donnell.

With these hands we are digging tunnels of sound.
Miners of the ear, we carve

> dwelling places for the imagination.

Don says, *Take this,* a voice
with coal dust on it, a story of texture and grain.

> He is the journeyman. I am apprentice.

I watch as his hands pick and shovel through the richness
of speech, material of breath.

> *Are you listening?* he asks. *Are you listening?*

It's a subtle stone we mine, subtle tools.
The workplace is quiet except for the lick and sizzle of voices,

> whisper of respirators, slow drip of groundwater.

We are digging a mine of no fixed address.
We will carry it with us, recording of small magics,

> we will return again and again.

AUTOBIOGRAPHY OF STONE

With thanks to Alice Otley

Shale, gneiss, granite, coal —
my names are as familiar
as rose, cedar, daisy.

You see me everywhere
and do not know me.
My parents are Rain and Sky.

What is stone
but earth fibre, rock juice,
potential?

To be the jealous cousin
little fits and yet
I envy the softness of bark,

easy transformation of leaves,
breath of sap,
the wider glance.

I am the oldest sister, arthritic,
cranky.
Wouldn't you?

I am fractured by light, heat, cold.
Every path is paved with stone.
Even a soft hand can be hard.

Trust me.
I am the root
to your wild.

CUEVA DEL INDIO, VINALES, CUBA

For Devon Ronner

It's a limestone cliff so eaten by rain and time that it hangs, a pale knitted shawl, over the lush of palms and tropical green in this country where mangos glow like Christmas tree decorations, common as pine cones, and purple and butter-yellow blossoms fall scattered like empty cups on the path to breakfast. On the first day she had gathered them, laid them on tables. Now, like other tourists, she steps over, doesn't even notice she has become reckless with beauty.

Years ago, the entrance to this cave was draped in foliage, a web of lianas and vines. Escaped natives, then slaves, hid here. Today the cave's mouth is bared to the sun and heavy beneath the weight of twelve stone steps. At the top a guitarist sings "Guantanamera" and waits for tourist pesos (dollars preferred). He barely nods at the one who drops only twenty-five cents in his basket because she wasn't paying attention, saw only the thin slice of dark behind him where the path enters the cave.

And she is inside the earth. It is cool here. It is no temperature at all. It is the temperature of the body. She forgets her skin, forgets she is separate. A damp in-drawn breath as rock above and around draws close, takes on the shape of wisps and fingers and threads slim as yellow candles. She walks through small chambers, channels so close she must duck and squeeze with the other tourists around stone carved by no man, until there is the smell and drip of water. A river. A boat.

When she steps forward, her vessel is flat and low. If she slips a hand over its rim, her fingers come back in trails of water, so she does not. She is not afraid, only holds to the side of the boat with one hand and sits very still while an old woman guides her along channels ever narrower, higher, deeper. She can't see the bottom of this strange river, looks up instead to fantastic shapes as the old woman names them: tobacco leaf, sea creature and skull. Seahorse and fish.

She can't shake this feeling of something familiar. Then a turn and light breaks open her eyes — a long bright slit, leaf-like, framed by darkness. The river floats toward it and the boat on the river and she inside. She cannot change it (her hand on the side of the boat, forgotten). She cannot change anything now as the boat passes through then suddenly it is day and hot here and a man extends one hand to help her from the boat and with his other extends the basket for tips and this time she drops in silver and paper but still she feels oddly lost and a little sad until someone slaps her gently on the bum and says, *You can breathe now. You're born again.* It's a joke. She laughs. But all the rest of that bright day she feels a little new, a little old, like a cup, fallen, almost shattered but found again, now whole and filled and beautiful.

Not a Labyrinth

Hungarian Ethnographic Museum, Budapest
with thanks to Seamus Heaney for "Crossings XXXI"

Not a labyrinth, not a cave,
for three hundred metres I follow
passages downward as if by torches

barely lit into quiet, still more quiet corridors
(no tourists here) following some olden thread
that leads me back through centuries

of medieval masonry, stone and rubble walls.
As if the hands of careful craftsmen push me further
over an aerial bridge, another stairway, down, stone

the only sound, my heart yearning to be small
between shadows. With every step, I bury myself
closer to the ones who dwell here, silent

citizens of another past now growing bold
seeing I come alone and empty-handed,
no pick or shovel with which to disturb them.

Stone chambers higher, heavier, brazen now
hint at a secret bloody history. Any minute
I shall hear it, out loud, in my living ears

when a doorway breaks, sudden light
spits me, breathless, through an archway
into the perfume of a rose-sweet garden

and a running fountain that trembles, sighing;
You are not the one we want today.
Go then. You can not stay.

The Door to Rock

> *the doors in us so closed, we think the door*
> *to rock is shut.*
>
> — Russell Thornton
> "The Oldest Rock in the World"

These three massive rocks, moss-covered,
that you so carelessly sat upon
for lunch (hadn't even asked them to be
your chair, your table, sandwiches spread)
suddenly vibrate, alive.

They shake in your seeing and shine,
three divinities sunk in velvet earth,
courtiers of green trees bending over
in slow conference.
How could there be such majesty?

You didn't know, not even suspect —
now your knees are weak with wanting
to fall, give rock its due, prostrate yourself
before inconceivable age, inconceivable wisdom
but instead

you turn with the others — foolish human —
and walk as directed into the hall
where you will sit
shimmering, your hands open
because now you know.

BLUE

> There's no thing that does not yearn.
>
> — Anne Michaels

Only a faint shadow here
where history seeps through blue granite walls,
a bittersweet salve.
Nothing of colour but dark,
no tapestry for warmth.
Here are the ghosts of those not invited.
This is the place where the child is not.

Some days she comes and sits and wails
in the company of wind.
There is solace in stone, a packed earth floor.
She raises her eyes to a ceiling of
midnight crystals lit from above,
jagged in a twilight hue.

This is a formal chamber,
place of shadows,
of a fierce, bare reckoning.
Mercy is inappropriate here.

Here is where a woman nourishes herself,
prepares for certain battle, eases herself
into other armors, keeps the dagger of her loss
hidden.

Stone gives her strength,
bare feet read the earth. She places them
one at a time, open
welcoming the sphere she walks on.
Clear blue, her cloak.

How To Homestead

For my grandmother, Sarah Baker, immigrant from Ireland to
Canada, 1905

*How do you grow a past
to live in?*

— Robert Kroetsch, "Seed Catalogue"

Plant stones. Water them
with sweat, tears,
anything salty.

Don't wear white.
It doesn't show
against snow.
Wear skirts, no matter what
common sense says.

Pray a lot.
To whom, is your own choice.
There has to be some advantage
to ending up in a _____
place like this.

Practise a local vernacular.
Listen for your own tongue.
Pretend you don't see the Cree,
the ones who came first.
Pretend you're alone.
Most of the time, you are.

Wiggle your roots. Lean
against trees
in between pulling out
as many as you can
in as short a time as possible.

After a while you can't hide
from the neighbours
(if you have any).

If you're a woman,
practise going crazy.

If you're a woman, of course
you'll have children
you'll have more children
you'll have

lots to do. At least
you won't be doing it alone.
If you live that long.

Look down.

Leave your hair,
your clothing, body fluids
at each of the four corners
of your world.

You'll have to start over
every damned day.
Do you hear me?

You'll have to have children.
If he doesn't beat you first.
Even then. Find the Cree.
They'll know what to do.

How long can you stay?
One hundred generations?
One?

Start with winter,
the worst one.
Try fire. Try sod.
Try freezing.

The voice of god, any god
won't heat a bloody tit in hell.
See that axe?
Dig right in. It's the beginning.

Don't be shy.

When the man dies
frozen somewhere between the house and the barn
you'll have to get rid of your skirts.

You never knew how warm,
having a good bit of wool
between your legs.

Pull the house closer,
the children, the chickens.
You're staying home tonight,
starting a new game.
Your move.

Pick up the rifle, the plow.
Tie a knot
in your end of the rope.
Take one step. Take one
loamy step. Another.

Plant stones.

THREE SMALL ROCKS BIG

By Georgia O'Keeffe, 1937
Oil on canvas

Here's a woman who doesn't fear hard edges,
small rocks that rattle and break
in the stone bowl of her heart.

When she is old
it will all be dust.

Innocent playthings,
three small pebbles found in the hills:
white for a polished tooth, rare pearl,
red for a half-sucked sweet

and black, where she hides
behind the pretty fence
of a hard steel frame.

THE BLESSING

It is a story I may not tell my grandchildren, how
in a Hungarian museum I wandered quite lost but

not worried really, an afternoon empty before me
to follow ever more ancient passageways, aged walls blackened
(by fire perhaps) and a bridge over stone-shimmering air, down.

How many years has it waited, this tiny chapel
buried in memory, the gold on the chandeliers now frayed,
blood-red rugs under how many holy, once noble feet?

I step to the stone alter rail and as if a hand fell suddenly
to my shoulder, I — non-Christian — drop
to my knees, echoing as if with voices

a song, my head pushed forward, bowed, not terrified only
in wonder, wanting to say hello to ghosts but
not speaking Latin, not knowing what else to do

but wait until the sound of soft slippers has passed,
the rustle of velvet so I can rise,
touch my lips to stone, singing.

YOU ARE A TRAVELLER STANDING IN FRONT OF A MOUNTAIN AND WERE JUST GOING TO SAY SOMETHING IMPORTANT

but it comes out of your mouth
a gravelly sound

and when you look —
mere stone

part of the larger community of rock
known for the silence of its speeches

the weight of its utterance,
long pauses.

You of the human shape
can't imagine the patience it takes.

It dances
a long grace, the O of a single round

well-considered word, a cave of silence
you enter.

Mouth and lips tingle.
Pressure now from the inside

out. Your heart slows
as you extend a hand, open

your mouth
to exclaim

but the time for that is over.

A small grey pebble rolls to the ground.
Another traveller passes it by.

We began
as a mineral. We emerged into plant life
and into animal state, and then into being human,
and always we have forgotten our former states,
except in early spring, when we slightly recall
being green again.

— Rumi

NOTES

In classical Western cosmology there are four elements — earth, water, air, fire — and a fifth, aether. I have taken the liberty of replacing aether with the classical Chinese element, wood.

Opening quote by D.H. Lawrence ("everything was alive…"), from "New Mexico" in *Survey Graphic*, May 1931, cited in *Georgia O'Keeffe in the West*. Ed. Doris Bry and Nicholas Callaway (NY: Knopf in association with Callaway, 1989), p. 7.

p. 14: *The Sunlit Sea Supports Nothing*. Epigraph from Guillaume Apollinaire in Catherine Owen, *The Wrecks of Eden*.

p. 15: *Tattoo*. Epigraph from Alice Oswald, "The Three Wise Men of Gotham Who Set Out to Catch the Moon in a Net" in *The Thing in the Gap-Stone Stile*.

p. 19: *Small Boat*. Epigraph from E.G. Burrows, "Milkweed."

p. 26: *Monolith*. Story of Amazon shamans' practice from Wade Davis' *One River*.

p. 29: *Lava*. Epigraph from Adrienne Rich, "For the Record" in *Poems 1982–1983*.

p. 31: *Opening the Cabin*. What the poet Jane Kenyon actually said was, "I am overcome // by ordinary contentment." In "Having it Out With Melancholy," in *Collected Poems*.

p. 36: *For Jude, the Cabinetmaker, in His Shop*. The forester in question, and source of some of this information, is Peter Wohlleben in *The Hidden Life of Trees: What They Feel, How They Communicate*.

p. 39: *Fairy Tale*. Epigraph from Linda Rogers' "Hot Air" in *Love in the Rain Forest*.

p. 41: *Masters of the Earth*. Epigraph from the Crosby, Stills and Nash song, "Déjà vu," words by David Crosby.

p. 42: *The Dimensions of Lumber.* An anchoress was a woman, often a nun, who chose for religious reasons to have herself sealed inside a stone wall or cave, with only an opening for food to be passed in.

p. 43: *Carpenter: To the Trees.* Epigraph from Lorna Crozier, "Table" in *Book of Marvels.*

p. 44: *Tree Song.* Epigraph from John Terpstra, "Naked Trees" in *Naked Trees.*

p. 46: *Grey.* The "Lawren" referred to is Lawren Harris, leader of the Canadian Group of Seven who when he first saw Emily Carr's work, told her, "You are one of us." He encouraged her to follow his own spiritual approach, called theosophy, that led to highly stylized portraits of nature. Emily later admitted the painting "Grey" was her last effort in that direction before returning to a more traditional spirituality and a less geometric approach to nature in her work.

p. 50: *Inside Mother Roof.* Traditional Japanese craftspeople are some of the world's greatest joiners (fine woodworkers), known for wood joins so tight yet so flexible that the nails and steel brackets common in the West are not necessary to hold huge beams together even in earthquakes. Each phrase here is the name of a different traditional join. All terms used were found in the glossary of *Japanese Joinery: A Handbook for Joiners and Carpenters* by Yasuo Nakahara (Cloudburst Press, 1983).

p. 56: *Redwing, I Say.* Epigraph from Maureen Scott Harris, "A Bird in the Hand: 5" in *Slow Curve Out.*

p. 60: *Crow: II.* Information on the Roman meaning of a crow's call, "Tomorrow, tomorrow," is from Barbara G. Walker, *The Woman's Dictionary of Symbols & Sacred Objects* (1988), p. 398.

p. 71: *Wood Buffalo National Park.* Epigraph from Sue Sinclair's "Big East Lake" in *Breaker.*

p. 73: *Moss and Stone.* Epigraph from Joseph Campbell as quoted in *Reflections on the Art of Living: A Joseph Campbell Companion.* Ed. Diane K. Osbon (NY: Harper Collins, 1991).

p. 81: *The Door to Rock.* Epigraph from Russell Thornton's "The Oldest Rock in the World" in *Birds, Metals, Stones & Rain.*

p. 82: *Blue*. Epigraph from Anne Michael's *Fugitive Pieces*.

p. 83: *How to Homestead*. Epigraph from Robert Kroetsch's "Seed Catalogue" in *Seed Catalogue*, reprinted from *Field Notes: The Collected Poetry of Robert Kroetsch*.

Acknowledgements

For readers interested in the use of traditional forms in poetry, in this collection there are two palindromes ("Empty Cup" and "Inside Mother Roof"), two glosas ("Fairy Tale" and "Tree Song"), a found poem ("Inside Mother Roof"), a variation of haibun ("She sits,") and several prose poems ("Airplane Whine," "Breath," "Calgary Stampede: 1956," "Blackberries for Jacqueline," and "Cueva del Indio"). For further information on these and many other forms, see *In Fine Form 2nd Edition: A Contemporary Look at Canadian Form Poetry,* Eds. Kate Braid and Sandy Shreve.

Poets are magpies, picking up ideas, images and suggestions everywhere, anywhere. But when it comes to pulling the resulting bits and poems together, certain people are essential. First, deepest thanks to Caitlin Press and the hard-working people there: Vici Johnstone, Michael Despotovic, Cara Cochrane and Emily Stringer. Without small presses like this, there would be no Canadian poetry. Special thanks to Marilyn Bowering and Sandy Shreve for wise eyes and kindly criticism, and to Dawn Kresan for (another) fine edit. Also thanks to my poetry group (Pam Galloway, Heidi Greco, Fiona Lam, Tana Runyan and Leslie Timmins). I am proud to be a member of the British Columbia poetry community — it's community that keeps me going.

My thanks also to the editors and staff of the journals and anthologies that first published some of these poems.

Catherines, the Great, Susie Berg, Ed. (Oolichan Press, 2018); *CV2* Summer 2009; *Event* 1997; *PRECIPICe*, Brock University, 2010; *Refugium: Poems for the Pacific.* Yvonne Blommer, Ed. (Caitlin, 2017); Federation of BC Writers *Wordworks* Spring 2017; *Arc* 1991; *Event,* April 2017; *In Fine Form 2nd Edition: A Contemporary Look at Canadian Form Poetry.* Eds. Kate Braid and Sandy Shreve (Caitlin, 2016); *The Fed Anthology: Brand New Fiction and Poetry From the Federation of BC Writers.* Ed. Susan Musgrave (Anvil, 2003); *Event,* 46/1, April 2017; *Descant Magazine; Room of One's Own; Arc Poetry Magazine; Prism International.*